YOU DON'T KNOW
JACK®

THE
TV
BOOK

Jellyvision™

BERKELEY
SYSTEMS

RUNNING PRESS
PHILADELPHIA · LONDON

© 1998 by Jellyvision, Inc.

You Don't Know Jack, Gibberish question, DisOrDat question, Screw Your Neighbor, Jack Attack, and the Jellyvision logo are registered trademarks or trademarks of Jellyvision, Inc. The Berkeley systems logo is a registered trademark of Berkeley Systems, Inc.

9 8 7 6 5 4 3 2 1

Digit on the right indicates the number of this printing

Library of Congress Cataloging-in-Publication Number 98-65175

ISBN 0-7624-0375-6

The "Jack Head" image is © Berkeley Systems, Inc.

Jellyvision Editor: David Nathanielsz
Lead Writer: Steven Heinrich
Questions Written By: The Jellyvision Writers

Designed by Maria Taffera Lewis
Edited by Brendan Cahill
Typography: Franklin Gothic

This book may be ordered by mail from the publisher.
Please include $2.50 for postage and handling.
But try your bookstore first!

Running Press Book Publishers
125 South Twenty-second Street
Philadelphia, Pennsylvania 19103-4399

Contents

introduction

Let's talk about you. You want to play. You're excited. Your bladder is as unstable as a deranged puppy out of medication. You're a trivia machine, and you're ready to produce.

Just settle down, Skippy. First you've got to know the rules.

QUESTION TYPES

This book is divided into several 10-question games, which you can play by yourself or with a group. Each game features four question types: Multiple-Choice, DisOrDat, Gibberish, and Jack Attack.

Multiple-Choice Questions There are seven Multiple-Choice questions in each game. They look something like this:

> **Based on the audience's famous name,**
> **which company would most likely sponsor the audience**
> **of the kids' show "Howdy Doody?"**
> **A. Tropicana™** **B. Domino's™**
> **C. Planter's™** **D. Oscar Meyer™**

The answer to this would be "C," because the name of "Howdy Doody's" audience was the "Peanut Gallery." See how that works? Of course you do. The answers to Multiple-Choice questions can be found by turning the page. It's quicker than going to the library to look it up yourself.

The Gibberish Question There's one Gibberish question in each game. The Gibberish phrase is a random series of words that rhyme with a well-known phrase. For example:

> **What phrase does this rhyme with?**
> **Loud jazz: the sea rock.**

You'll find the real phrase on the next page. In this case, the answer is: **Proud as a Peacock**. We'll give you a few hints to help you out, but no Multiple-Choice answers. Got it? Super.

The DisOrDat Question In each game, there is a seven-point DisOrDat question. Take a look at this:

**Below are seven TV monkeys. For each one,
identify if it's a real primate or an animated primate.**

1. Grape Ape	2. Mr. Smith
3. Lancelot Link	4. Chim Chim
5. Gleek	6. The Bear

7. The Marquis Chimps

You just decide if it's one or the other. In this case, Mr. Smith, The Bear, and The Marquis Chimps are real monkeys; Grape Ape, Lancelot Link, Chim Chim, and Gleek are animated monkeys. The answers to DisOrDats are found at the end of each game.

In some DisOrDats, one answer fits both of the categories. If there are going to be some answers that are both, we'll let you know at the beginning. We're just nice that way.

The Jack Attack At the end of each game there is a Jack Attack. For each Jack Attack, you want to correctly match the root words with the corresponding matching phrase. The correct matches should be based on the category on the top of the page.

For example, if your Jack Attack clue is **We Make Beautiful Music Together,** you might see **David Letterman** and match him with **Paul Shaffer.** You'd be right, and that'd be just swell. But then you might see **Johnny Carson** and match him with **Ed McMahon.** Then you'd be wrong, and you'd feel stupid. Johnny's band leader was **Doc Severinson,** not Ed. See?

Jack Attack answers are found at the end of each game.

SCORING

Whether you're playing by yourself or with a group of people, the best way to play *You Don't Know Jack* is competitively. So we've provided you with an easy-to-learn scoring system. If you're playing competitively, it's best to have paper and pencils handy for scoring. It's even better if you all get inside a big steel cage and lock the door.

■ Each **Multiple-Choice Question** is worth two points.

■ **DisOrDats** are worth a total of seven points. For each DisOrDat question you get right, give yourself one point. And a little love.

■ The **Gibberish Question,** if you can figure out what the Gibberish phrase rhymes without the help of a hint, you get four points. If you need one hint, take three points. Two hints, two points. Using all three hints gets you a single point. And if you still can't figure it out after all the hints, you get nothing. Nada. Zilch.

■ In the **Jack Attack,** each correctly paired root and match is worth two points. That's a total of 14 points, which means if you really stink at all the other questions, you can still feel like you have a chance to win it all in the Jack Attack round. You don't, but it's still a nice feeling.

If you don't understand a question, skip it and never come back. It's just over your head and that's not going to change.

PLAYING WITH YOURSELF

If you can't figure out how to play this by yourself, perhaps you need a simpler hobby. Have you ever considered macramé?

Each game ends with a ratings chart. You can compare your score with the chart to find out just how stupid you are.

PLAYING WITH A GROUP

First, get a few friends together. At least one. If you can't do that, start working on your personality. Try to be a better listener. Don't be afraid to be vulnerable.

It's easiest if one person is host for each game, so pick one. We suggest choosing the most attractive person in the room. You're all going to be looking at the host for the next fifteen minutes, so it's best if he or she is not an eyesore.

Next, decide if you want to have individual players or teams. If you've got more than three players you should make teams. It's better that way. Trust us.

The host should write the players' or teams' names down on a sheet of paper. Each player/team should come up with a different "buzzer" sound. The human noises meant to represent barnyard animals work well as buzzer sounds, because they're easily distinguished. It's also an opportunity to realize how those noises sound nothing like the real animals.

For the Multiple-Choice questions the host should read off the category, the question and all Multiple-Choice answers. Host: Don't giggle while you do this. We spent a lot of time writing these questions so don't screw them up with your delivery.

As soon as the host is done reading, the players can buzz in by "mooing" or "clucking" or whatever it is, while frantically waving their arms. The host should take a minute to appreciate how idiotic they look, then call on the person who buzzed in first.

If they get it right, the host gives that player/team two points by drawing two chicken-scratch marks under their name. (That's right, chicken-scratch marks . . . notice the barnyard metaphor is holding.)

If they miss it, we highly encourage taunting. Then, allow any of the other players to cluck in. And so on, until somebody gets it right. If no one gets it right, tell them the right answer and read the corresponding comments. Try to be funny while doing this; no one likes a boring game-show host.

For Gibberish questions, the host should read the category and the Gibberish phrase. If after five seconds nobody's buzzed in, the host should read the first clue for the idiot players. Every five seconds the host should read another clue. If nobody gets it after the final clue has been read then move on and nobody gets any points. Oh, and one person must die.* It's the rules. Don't question them.

For the DisOrDat every player or team should have a pencil and some paper. As the host reads the DisOrDat, the players should write down their responses to each of the seven items. After all seven have been read, players should pass their answers to the player or team to the right and the host can read the answers.

The Jack Attack is the final part of the game. Each player/team gets sixty seconds to view the Jack Attack page and write down the seven matches. The host can keep time by using a stopwatch, or stamping his or her foot like a horse sixty times. After all players/teams have had their turn, they again pass their answers to the right and the host reads the correct matches for the Jack Attack.

> ## STUMPED?
> ### THEN SCREW YOUR NEIGHBOR!
>
> If you don't know the answer to a Multiple-Choice question—or know that one of your opponents doesn't— you can buzz in, say "Screw 'Em" and force them to answer the question. If your opponent doesn't get the answer, they lose two points. If they get it right, they get two points and you lose two points. But remember, you can only screw on Multiple-Choice questions and you can only do it once per game, so screw wisely.

The host then totals up the points and announces the winner. Thumb wrestle to break any tie. No, wait—the two players should urinate in different parts of the room to mark off barnyard territory while making their clucking or mooing sounds, and then fight to the death! Yeah, that's it.

Finally, if you don't like these rules, change them. If you have an aversion to barnyard animals, imitate a choo-choo train. Really, we just don't care, because whatever you do, YOU DON'T KNOW JACK!

* Don't actually kill someone, you sicko.

Game

1

THE TRUTH IS STRANGER
THAN JERRY SPRINGER

Because he was the city's real-life
mayor when the show debuted,
on which show should Jerry
Springer have done a cameo?

- **a** "Miami Vice™"
- **b** "Dallas™"
- **c** "WKRP in Cincinnati"
- **d** "L.A. Law"

Butt a What?

Which major network did NOT produce an Amy Fisher story?

- **a** ABC™
- **b** NBC™
- **c** CBS™
- **d** FOX™

Question 3 — Yum! Lemon Rinds!

Gibberish Question

With what phrase does this rhyme?

Flickerfish Nosescum

The rind is the bearable zing you taste.

Hint 1
It was in a
commercial during
the '80s.

Hint 2
The United Negro College
Fund™ used this message.

Hint 3
Your brain is a bad thing to throw away.

Answer 1

C

"WKRP in Cincinnati" premiered in 1978 and Jerry Springer was Cincinnati's mayor from 1977 to 1981. Jerry Springer was elected mayor after resigning from the city council for being caught paying a prostitute with a check. And you thought his *show* was stupid . . .

Answer 2

ABC™, CBS™ and NBC™ all produced Amy Fisher stories, and the only network to show some taste was FOX™. Which may mark the first time the words "FOX™" and "show some taste" have been used in the same sentence.

Answer 3: Gibberish Question

A mind is a terrible thing to waste.

Yep, a mind is a terrible thing to waste. That's why it's good to spend your time reading

b. "Where Was I?"

c. "Where'd You Go?"

d. "What's Going On?"

Question 5

It's a Beautiful Day in the Cubicle

If Mister Rogers wanted to be on a show that resembled his job
before hosting "Mister Rogers' Neighborhood™," on which show would he
MOST LIKELY want to work?

a "Amen™"

b "Welcome Back, Kotter"

c "The White Shadow"

d "Taxi™"

Question 6

But if Jean Stapleton Starts Singing, I'm Outta Here!

Suppose the cast of "All in the Family™" is having an extended family
reunion and the casts of all the shows it spawned are invited to attend.
Which show's cast would NOT be invited?

a "Gloria"

b "Alice"

c "Maude™"

d "The Jeffersons™"

11

Answer 4

c

"Where'd You Go?"
was never a TV game show.
They made the pilot, but it ran away.

Answer 5

Mr. Rogers is an actual ordained minister, so he'd be at home with "Amen™"'s ministers and deacons. *"And the Lord said, 'Let there be sweaters, trolleys, and puppets.' And the Lord saw that this was good. Can I get a positive affirmation from the congregation?"*

Answer 6

b

"Alice" is the only show listed that was not a spin-off from "All in the Family™." So the phrase "Kiss my Meathead" is destined not to be uttered on TV. Well, maybe on cable.

Question 7

TV on Your Back

Complete this "Tonight Show" sequence:

Steve Allen, _____, _____, _____, Jay Leno

a. Jack Paar, Johnny Carson, David Letterman

b. Jack Lescoulie, Jack Paar, Johnny Carson

c. Merv Griffin, Johnny Carson, Joan Rivers

d. Jack Benny, Dick Cavett, Johnny Carson

Question 8

A PARTNERSHIP MADE IN HELL

Complete this TV math problem:

the old detective from "Barney Miller"
+ Officer Poncherello =

a) Wojo and the Man

b) Fish and CHiPs

c) Yemana on the John

d) Ponch and Judy

Question 9

Zoinks! Forsooth!

Which of the following is NOT true about BOTH Hamlet and Scooby Doo™?

a.
They both spend a lot of time in castles.

b.
They both know someone named Daphne.

c.
They both see ghosts.

d.
They're both great Danes.

Answer 7

b

THE HOSTS OF NBC™'S "THE TONIGHT SHOW™," IN ORDER, ARE STEVE ALLEN, JACK LESCOULIE, JACK PAAR, JOHNNY CARSON, AND JAY LENO. THAT'S IF YOU DON'T COUNT THOSE STRANGE GALLAGHER YEARS.

Answer 8

b

Fish from "Barney Miller" and Ponch from "CHiPs". That'd make a great show—they could even have a street-wise informant named Malt Vinegar.

Answer 9

b

Only Scooby knew Daphne; the gal in Hamlet's life is Ophelia. Now you can feel cultured when you're watching Saturday morning cartoons in your underwear.

This Goes Far Beyond Pat

Male or Female?

1. Dobie Gillis

2. Fibber McGee

3. D.J. Tanner

4. Bat Masterson

5. Six LeMuere

6. Nurse Curly Spaulding

7. Ponder Blue

Nice Hair, Dork

pageboy

ducktail

2. Marge Simpson

curls

Homer

4. Sergeant Carter

hairspray

mousse

dreadlocks

shag

6. Laura Petrie

beard

French braid

toupee

wisps

bald

extensions

1. Cindy Brady

blue beehive

pompadour

3. Fonzie

hair weave

Mohawk

Aaaaaaay!

5. Keith Partridge

bowl cut

bob

7. Bull Shannon

flip

crew cut

DisOrDat Answer

1. Dobie Gillis / *male*

2. Fibber McGee / *male*

3. D.J. Tanner / *female*

4. Bat Masterson / *male*

5. Six LeMuere / *female*

6. Nurse Curly Spaulding / *female*

7. Ponder Blue / *male*

Jack Attack Answers

1. *Cindy Brady/ curls*

2. *Marge Simpson/ blue beehive*

3. *Fonzie/ ducktail*

4. *Sergeant Carter/ crew cut*

5. *Keith Partridge/ shag*

6. *Laura Petrie/ flip*

7. *Bull Shannon/ bald*

Rate Your Score

36 points or better: Okay.
Not completely idiotic.

30–35 points: Eh.
Some idiotic moments.

20–29 points: Pretty bad.
*This is about what we'd expect
an idiot to do.*

10–19 points: L'idiot.
That's French for "idiot."

0–9 points: You win!
*And if you scored this low,
you probably believe that.*

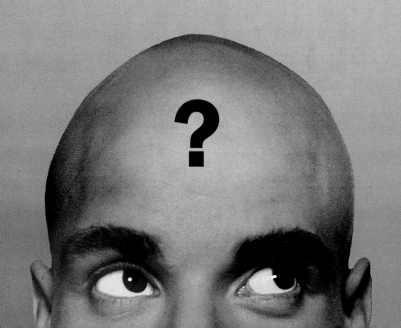

Game

2

Your Question, Should You Choose To Accept It

Suppose you receive one of those "mission tapes" as seen on the show "Mission Impossible." Which of these would you have EXACTLY enough time to do between the end of the "mission tape" and the time that it self-destructs?

a) recount your nipples, one per second

b) catch three seconds of a Tony Robbins speech

c. microwave a five-second tofu "power snack"

d. reenact a 10-second space shuttle countdown

Question 2

Hey! Where Did That Doo Come From?

If Scooby were to adopt the name of the person indirectly responsible for the name "Scooby Doo™," what would Scooby's new name be?

a.
Scooby Doo™ Sinatra

b.
CBS™ President Scoobert "Scooby" Dugan

c.
Scooby Dick Nixon

d.
Scooby "Mushmouth" Doo

Question 3

ONE OF THESE THINGS IS NOT LIKE THE OTHERS

Which of these does not equal six?

a) Brady kids

b) "Charlie's Angels™" over five seasons

c) Walton children

d) categories in a Double Jeopardy!™ round

The mission tapes on "Mission: Impossible" always self-destruct in five seconds, just enough time to reheat some tofu.

"And Jim, whatever you do, remember this one thing: depending on the size of your microwave, heating times may vary. Good luck, Jim."

Answer 2

CBS'™ FRED SILVERMAN HEARD **SINATRA'S SONG** "STRANGERS IN THE NIGHT," AND GOT SCOOB'S NAME **FROM THE LINE** "SCOOBY DOOBY DOO . . ." **IT'S A GOOD THING** HE WASN'T LISTENING TO THE **BUTTHOLE SURFERS AT THE TIME.**

Answer 3

There are seven Walton

kids. Plus, you gotta count

that giant mole on John

Boy's face. That's half a kid

right there.

Question 4

Low Flying Nun

Let's say the head of the FAA grounds the Flying Nun due to faulty mechanics. Based on her flying mechanism, how might the report read?

a. "internal jet pack: frozen"
b. "coronet: cracked"
c. "one magic clog: missing"
d. "lost faith in: God"

Question 5

Dead Clown Walking

On a famous episode of "The Mary Tyler Moore Show™," Chuckles the Clown dies. Given the cause of Chuckles' tragic death, what song would be MOST inappropriate to play at his funeral?

a "Great Balls of Fire"
b "Muskrat Love"
c "Baby Elephant Walk"
d "Little Red Corvette"

Question 6 — More Fun on the Set of "Saved by the Bell™"

Gibberish Question

With what phrase does this rhyme?

Screech bowled epithet free.

Hint **1**
You hear it in TV ads.

Hint **2**
It's said at the end of toy commercials.

Hint **3**
Most of the stuff is not sold together.

Answer 4

b Whenever a stiff wind blows in the convent, the flying nun is lifted off the ground by her winged hat, or coronet. You know, the best thing about Flying Nun Airlines is all the flight attendants are single.

Answer 5

C. CHUCKLES THE CLOWN WAS KILLED BY AN ELEPHANT WHILE DRESSED AS A GIANT PEANUT. WHICH JUST GOES TO SHOW: NEVER BECOME A CLOWN AND THEN GET DRESSED UP LIKE A GIANT PEANUT AND THEN GET KILLED BY AN ELEPHANT.

Answer 6: Gibberish Question

each sold separately

What they should have said is, "there's no way you'll ever have as much fun with all these toys as these actors are having."

Question 7

Aren't You a Little Hairy for a Villain?

Oh no! There's a werewolf on the loose in TV Land! Because of the type of weapon he or she uses, which of these TV law-enforcers would make the best werewolf hunter?

a.
the Six Million Dollar Man™

b.
Wonder Woman™

c.
T.J. Hooker

d.
the Lone Ranger™

Question 8

DROP THE HERRING, DIRTBAG!

Because of the origin of the phrase "Five-O," what would be a logical name for a show based on "Hawaii Five-O" but set in Alaska?

a | "Alaska Four-Nine"

b | "Baked Alaska"

c | "Alaska 10-4"

d | "Alaska Five-AB Negative"

Question 9

Goof Nutrition & the Little Rascals

Which of these is NOT both a grain and a member of "Our Gang™"?

a. Buckwheat

b. Barley

c. Farina

d. Alfalfa

d The Lone Ranger uses silver bullets, which is what you need to kill a werewolf. He used to carry a crucifix and some garlic, but he couldn't get the criminals to stop laughing.

The "Five-O" refers to Hawaii being the 50th state. And Alaska is the 49th state. So it'd be "Alaska Four-Nine."

"Bb-b-b-b-book 'im, Dd-d-d-danno."

BARLEY. IT'S NOT AN "OUR GANG™" MEMBER BUT IT IS A GRAIN THAT'S EATEN OFTEN. DARLA ON THE OTHER HAND, WELL . . . YOU GET THE PICTURE.

I Hate You–
Now Come to Bed

"Dallas™" or "Dynasty"?

1. Blake

2. J.R.

3. Alexis

4. Miss Ellie

5. Krystle

6. Digger

7. Fallon

Jack Attack

Everything Was Fine Until You Came Along

Gopher

1. "The Brady Bunch™"

Scrappy

3. "Mork & Mindy"

Tiger

4. "Family Ties™"

Cuba

baby

Pebbles

6. "The Flintstones™"

Pacific Princess™

Oliver

Gloria

Isaac

Mearth little Ricky

Andy

Promenade Deck

2. "The Love Boat™"

ghost

Fred

Shaggy

Jennifer

5. "Scooby Doo™"

Orson

Vicki

brother

7. "I Love Lucy™"

Scooter

Ethel

DisOrDat Answer

1. Blake / "*Dynasty*"
2. J.R. / "*Dallas*™"
3. Alexis / "*Dynasty*"
4. Miss Ellie / "*Dallas*™"
5. Krystle / "*Dynasty*"
6. Digger / "*Dallas*™"
7. Fallon / "*Dynasty*"

Jack Attack Answers

1. *"The Brady Bunch™" / Oliver*
2. *"The Love Boat™" / Vicki*
3. *"Mork & Mindy" / Mearth*
4. *"Family Ties™" / Andy*
5. *"Scooby Doo™" / Scrappy*
6. *"The Flintstones™" / Pebbles*
7. *"I Love Lucy™" / little Ricky*

Rate Your Score

36 points or better: Nice work. *We'll call you "Mercurio," because that sounds like a smart person.*

30–35 points: "Hardy." *Because you're half mystery-solving youth/ half overweight comedian.*

20–29 points: You're "Doobie." *Accept it.*

10–19 points: "Tess." *It kind of rhymes with "ass," but not really.*

0–9 points: "Pauly." *Just "Pauly."*

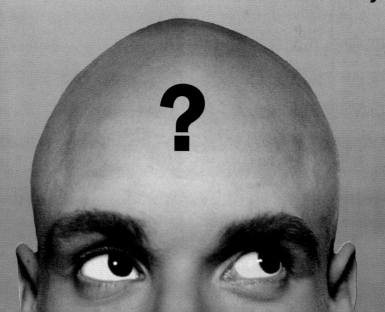

Game

3

Where's the Fifth Dimension on This Damn Map?!

According to the show's introductions, which of these is a place where "The Twilight Zone™" exists?

a between science and superstition
b between the conscious and the subconscious
c between reality and illusion
d between "Roc™" and "Melrose Place™"

You Go, Girl! Woof!

Imagine that the dog who played Lassie™ is booked to appear on "The Ricki Lake Show." Which of these might be the topic for that show?

a. "I made 20 films and I'm dog tired!"

b. "Help! I'm blind and nobody knows it!"

c. "Everybody thinks I'm a bitch, but I'm not!"

d. "I gave birth to another TV dog's puppy!"

There's No Such Thing as Too Much Caffeine

Oh, no! Aliens have destroyed your local Starbucks™! Given their long-standing hatred of things named Starbuck, which evil aliens are the MOST likely suspects?

Answer 1

A. ACCORDING TO ROD SERLING, "THE TWILIGHT ZONE™" IS "THE MIDDLE GROUND BETWEEN LIGHT AND SHADOW, SCIENCE AND SUPERSTITION."

KIND OF LIKE UTAH.

Answer 2

c

"Everybody thinks I'm a bitch, but I'm not!"

A bitch is a female dog and though six different dogs played the female canine Lassie, not a single one was female. No wonder Lassie always peed standing up.

Answer 3

a

On Battlestar Galactica, The Cylon Raiders™ fight Lieutenant Starbuck. He eventually defeats them by charging way too much for a decaf latté.

Question 4

Marcia & Her Tight End

Complete this analogy:
Marcia Brady is to football as:

a.
Elmer Fudd™
is to wabbit

b.
Geraldo Rivera
is to chair

c.
Ted Danson
is to hairpiece

d.
Mr. Rogers
is to sweater

Question 5

DOES THAT LI'L DOOFUS HAVE A BROADCASTING DEGREE?

Ratings for "The Today Show" soared in 1953 when NBC™ added J. Fred Muggs to the show. If a TV movie were made about the life of J. Fred Muggs, what might it be called?

(a) "Me and Mr. Microphone™: A Child's Story"

(b) "A Reporter Unleashed: A Dog's Story"

(c) "And the Swinging Stopped: A Chimp's Story"

(d) "Stage Lights Melt Plastic: A Puppet's Story"

Question 6 — Werewolf-Like Symptoms

Gibberish Question

What does this rhyme with? Flickernish Nosescum

hairy, lathers, has the fever

Hint 1
You hear this at the beginning of a classic show.

Hint 2
It's from the credits of "Leave it to Beaver."

Hint 3
Gee, Wally . . . who plays the Beaver?

Answer 4

MARCIA BRADY GOT HIT IN THE NOSE **WITH A FOOTBALL,** WHILE GERALDO GOT HIT IN THE NOSE, **ON HIS TV SHOW,** WITH A FLYING CHAIR.

"NOW THE DYSFUNCTIONAL TRANSVESITE **UNWED MOTHERS** WILL NEVER ASK ME TO THE PROM!"

Answer 5

J. Fred Muggs was a broadcasting monkey.

The first of many.

Answer 6: Gibberish Question

Jerry Mathers as "The Beaver"

The Beaver: the kid who escaped more punishments than a savings-and-loan officer in

If I Had a Battery up My Butt I'd Move like That, Too

Because this TV show keeps going and going longer than any other, on which show would the Energizer Bunny™ be an appropriate guest?

a. "Meet the Press™"

b. "The Tonight Show™"

c. "Oprah™"

d. "Larry King Live™"

Question 8

WATERGATE & CABLE TV

Suppose while being arrested, the Watergate burglars had claimed to be cable guys. Since this network began in 1972, the year of the burglary, which channel could they have been installing?

a. CNN™

b. ESPN™

c. HBO™

d. MTV™

Question 9

Birds, Bees, & "The Simpsons™"

Imagine this:
On a very special episode of "The Simpsons™," Homer explains to Bart where he came from. What will Homer most likely say?

a.
"The funny pages, boy."

b.
"Public access, boy."

c.
"'Liquid Television™,' boy."

d.
"'The Tracey Ullman Show,' boy."

37

Answer 7

a

"MEET THE PRESS™," THE LONGEST RUNNING SHOW ON TELEVISION, HAS BEEN ON THE AIR SINCE 1947. AFTER 50 YEARS, YOU'D THINK WE'D HAVE MET THE PRESS BY NOW. BUT NO, THE SHOW KEEPS GOING...

Answer 8

c

In 1972, Home Box Office™ premiered by showing Paul Newman's film "Sometimes a Great Notion." Although the cover never would have worked. Who would believe that the cable guys actually showed up?

Answer 9

d

"The Tracy Ullman Show" gave "The Simpsons™" a weekly showcase before it broke off to become its own show. Bart always just assumed he fell out of his mom's hair.

Keep a Stiff Upper Lip

Mustache or No Mustache?

1. Archie Bunker

2. Gomez Addams

3. Thomas Magnum

4. Isaac Washington

5. Ricky Ricardo

6. Barney Miller

7. Gabe Kotter

Jack Attack

Sing Along
if You Must

1. "The Jeffersons™"

"Those Were the Days"

3. "M*A*S*H™"

"Marry Me" *"War Is Funny"*

4. "All in the Family™"

lame show *Hawkeye*

"Movin' on Up"

"Love & Marriage"

Chandler

7. "Family Ties™"

tone-deaf

"The Facts of Life"

"Gloria"

"Suicide Is Painless"

2. "Friends™"

"Welcome Back"

"Bundy's Theme"

"Our Lives Suck"

"We're All Learnin'"

5. "Married with Children"

"Superfly"

"I'll Be There for You"

6. "The Facts of Life™"

"Without Us"

"Deluxe Apartment"

DisOrDat Answer

1. Archie Bunker/*no mustache*

2. Gomez Addams/*mustache*

3. Thomas Magnum/*mustache*

4. Isaac Washington/*mustache*

5. Ricky Ricardo/*no mustache*

6. Barney Miller/*mustache*

7. Gabe Kotter/*mustache*

Jack Attack Answers

1. "The Jeffersons™"/"Movin' on Up"

2. "Friends™"/ "I'll Be There for You"

*3. "M*A*S*H™"/ "Suicide Is Painless"*

4. "All in the Family™"/ "Those Were the Days"

5. "Married with Children"/ "Love & Marriage"

6. "The Facts of Life™"/ "The Facts of Life"

7. "Family Ties™"/ "Without Us"

Rate Your Score

36 points or better: Congratulations.
You've won nothing.

30–35 points: Almost perfect.
Einstein got some things wrong
. . . like that haircut.

20–29 points: Unimpressive.
Sorry, didn't mean to remind you
about your life right now.

10–19 points: You tried.
But a trained monkey
could have done better.

0–9 points: Just move on.
For you, we wouldn't even have
to train the monkey.

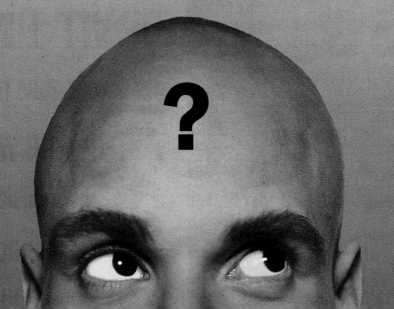

Game

4

DON'T CALL ME "MISTER"

Which of the following TV "misters" is NOT a teacher?

a Mr. Novak from "Mr. Novak"

b. Mr. Peepers from "Mr. Peepers"

c Mr. Sunshine from "Mr. Sunshine"

d Mr. Smith from "Mr. Smith"

Wonder Woman™ & Haute Couture

In the theme song to the '70s TV show "Wonder Woman™," how is Wonder Woman™ described?

a.
"in your satin tights, fighting for your rights"

b.
"in your lycra™ suit, daring thugs to shoot"

c.
"in your killer pumps, taking all your lumps"

c.
"in your bustier, making bad guys pay"

Question 3 — People Who Really Hate Seafood

Gibberish Question

With what TV phrase does this rhyme? *Flickerfish Nosescum*

Vile cur! Prawn? Canned Squid? Damn ya!

Hint 1
A stranger might say this to you.

Hint 2
They'd say it after you've been made the butt of a practical joke.

Hint 3
Let's be candid. You've got a good smile.

Answer 1

d

Mr. Smith is an orangutan with an IQ of 256 who works for the government. Which isn't that odd, really. They're used to monkeys in Washington.

Answer 2

"IN YOUR SATIN TIGHTS, FIGHTING FOR YOUR RIGHTS." ONE OF THE MOST RIDICULOUS SONG LYRICS OF ALL TIME. UNLESS YOU COUNT ANYTHING BY JEFFERSON STARSHIP™

Answer 3: Gibberish Question

Smile!
You're on "Candid Camera"!

Remember that "Candid Camera" episode
with Rob Lowe?
Wasn't that great?

Mailmen Who Really Deliver

There's a rumor going around that your mother had an affair with the mailman!
If the rumors are true, which TV character's features
could you NOT have inherited?

- a. Cliff Clavin's annoying personality
- b. Newman's good looks
- c. Ralph Kramden's temper
- d. Mr. McFeely's legs

Question 5

A Report Card Full of A-Teams

If the "B.A." on your college diploma stands for the same thing as the "B.A." in B.A.
Baracus from "The A-Team," in what did you earn your degree?

a. "Big Arms"
b. "Bad Attitude"
c. "Bright Amulets"
d. "Bodacious Artillery"

Question 6

Hubellubo, Jason Priestly!

Imagine that, due to low ratings, "Beverly Hills 90210™" moves to
zip code 02134, home of the '70s kids' show "Zoom™." In "Ubbi-Dubbi,"
how might the 90210 cast respond to its new hometown?

a. "Wube hubate Bubostubon!"
b. "Wube hubate Chubucubagubo!"
c. "Wube hubate Nubew Yubork!"
d. "Wube hubate Pubarubis!"

Ralph Kramden's not a mailman, he's a bus driver. But if he pays the fare, maybe your mom'll take him for a ride.

Answer 5

"BAD ATTITUDE."

GUESS YOU SHOULDN'T HAVE REFERRED TO ALL YOUR PROFESSORS AS "FOOL."

Answer 6

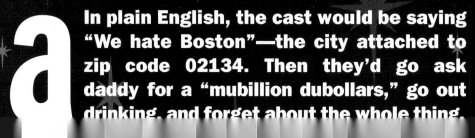

In plain English, the cast would be saying "We hate Boston"—the city attached to zip code 02134. Then they'd go ask daddy for a "mubillion dubollars," go out drinking, and forget about the whole thing.

Set Phasers to "Boogie"

Suppose the crew of the Starship Enterprise™ is so incredibly bored that they decide to form a rock band. Since they also had a show based in space, which band could the crew call upon for music lessons?

a. Josie and the Pussycats™

b. the Archies™

c. California Dreams™

d. the Monkees™

LET'S KEEP IT BRIEFS

If you want to pretend you're "The Greatest American Hero," what would you have to wear while jumping off your roof?

a) your "tightie-whities"

b) your "nothin's"

c) your "jammies"

d) your "jumper"

I'm Not a Wrestler, but I Play One on TV

Complete this analogy:

High school wrestling is to professional wrestling as:

a. "The Late Show" is to "The Tonight Show."

b. "People's Court™" is to "Divorce Court."

c. "M*A*S*H™" is to Dr. Quinn.

d. ESPN™ is to CNN™.

a

"JOSIE & THE PUSSYCATS™" BECAME "JOSIE & THE PUSSYCATS IN OUTER SPACE™" IN 1972.

"CAPTAIN, SLAMMING THE MICROPHONE STAND TO THE FLOOR AFTER THE GUITAR RIFF IS HIGHLY ILLOGICAL, THOUGH IT IS INDEED MOST RADICAL."

Answer 8

On "The Greatest American Hero," Robert Culp refers to William Katt's superhero suit as the "jammies." Just make sure your "jammies" are clean when you jump off the roof. You don't want your mother to be too embarrassed when they scrape you off the pavement.

Answer 9

b "Divorce Court" is a dramatization by actors. High school wrestling is an actual sport, while professional wrestling is, well, you know. Other similarities: a lot of women in divorce court would like to "pile-drive" their husbands, and Judge Wapner would look really cute in a blue bodysuit.

Son, Your Father and I Have Something to Tell You . . .

Adopted or Not Adopted?

1. Danny Partridge

2. Rudy Huxtable

3. Webster

4. John Boy Walton

5. Gloria Bunker

6. Arnold Drummond

7. Ernie Douglas

We Haven't Seen Hide nor Hair of Them

Laura

Charlie

2. "Rhoda"

Cliff

Niles' wife, Maris

Brenda

4. "Charlie Brown Christmas™"

Lilith

humor

Macaulay Culkin

"The Bad Seed"

Norm's wife, Vera

7. "Cheers™"

Lou Grant

Wilson

Seattle skyline

1. "Charlie's Angels™"

Rebecca

Carlton, the doorman

Agent Cooper

Brendan

3. "Twin Peaks"

Diane, the secretary

adults

wore bandages

Herman

5. "Home Improvement"

Farrah

6. "Frasier™"

Roz

Rigid Tool™ Girl

DisOrDat Answer

1. Danny Partridge / *not adopted*
2. Rudy Huxtable / *not adopted*
3. Webster / *adopted*
4. John Boy Walton / *not adopted*
5. Gloria Bunker / *not adopted*
6. Arnold Drummond / *adopted*
7. Ernie Douglas / *adopted*

Jack Attack Answers

1. *"Charlie's Angels™" / Charlie*
2. *"Rhoda" / Carlton, the doorman*
3. *"Twin Peaks" / Diane, the secretary*
4. *"Charlie Brown Christmas™" / adults*
5. *"Home Improvement" / Wilson*
6. *"Frasier™" / Niles' wife, Maris*
7. *"Cheers™" / Norm's wife, Vera*

Rate Your Score

36 points or better: Marcia Brady.
*You're like the prettiest,
most popular one.*

30–35 points: Greg Brady
*Not quite Marcia,
but your jeans are far out.*

20–29 points: Sam the butcher.
*Nothing overwhelming, just a human being
happy to be surrounded by quality meat.*

10–19 points: Cindy Brady.
*Cute, but your answers are
unintelligible.*

0–9 points: Oliver.
When you arrive, people know the end is near.

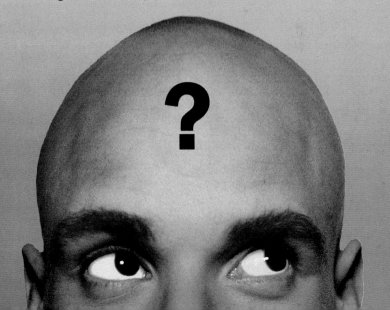

Game

5

Great Moments in Television Programming

Which of these was NOT an actual television series?

a. "The Ugliest Girl in Town"

b. "The Girl with Something Extra"

c. "Torso the Clown"

d. "My Mother the Car"

Question 2

ALL I'VE GOT ARE TWO LINTBALLS AND A USED CONDOM

Which TV character's trash is this?
A roll of duct tape, a bent paper clip,
a packet of Alka-Seltzer™, a Swiss
Army knife and a business card that
says "The Phoenix Foundation."

a | Bob Vila

b | MacGyver

c | Maxwell Smart

d | Steve Austin

Question 3

Soft Drink Espionage

Which one of the
following celebrities
could be executed for treason
as a double agent
of the cola wars?

a.
Ray Charles

b.
Madonna

c.
Michael Jackson

d.
David Bowie

C

"TORSO THE CLOWN" WAS NOT A SERIES. THE CENSORS THOUGHT IT MIGHT FRIGHTEN THE CHILDREN. PLUS, THERE WAS REALLY ONLY ONE PLACE HE COULD WEAR THAT BIG RED NOSE.

Answer 2

MacGyver works for the Phoenix Foundation and saves the day by using trash like duct tape, paper clips, and Alka Seltzer™. You know what they say: one man's trash is another man's thermonuclear warhead.

Answer 3

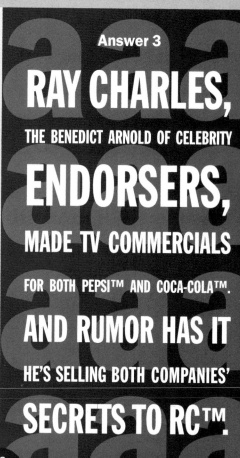

RAY CHARLES, THE BENEDICT ARNOLD OF CELEBRITY ENDORSERS, MADE TV COMMERCIALS FOR BOTH PEPSI™ AND COCA-COLA™. AND RUMOR HAS IT HE'S SELLING BOTH COMPANIES' SECRETS TO RC™.

WHOA!

Say your life is already filled with so much woe that you must avoid any show with that "Whoa!" guy, Joey Lawrence, on it. Which of these sitcoms can you watch?

a) "Gimme a Break"

b) "Growing Pains"

c) "Blossom"

d) "Brotherly Love"

Mr. Fonzarelli Will See You Now

Suppose Fonzie's accused of stealing office supplies from his own "office." Which of these items would most likely be used as evidence?

a.
engine lube

b.
ketchup

c.
LP records

d.
urinal cakes

Gibberish Question

With what phrase does this rhyme?

Sin? Dare me go bear the jail trouble.

Hint 1

This is shown on screen before a show.

Hint 2

It informs you of the sound quality.

Hint 3

If you're lucky, it won't be in mono.

Answer 4

b Joey Lawrence was never part of the cast of "Growing Pains." And if you're watching one of Joey Lawrence's actual programs, you can be sure your brain will not experience any growing pains.

Answer 5

d Fonzie's office is the men's bathroom at Arnold's Drive-in. The office decor isn't the best, but it's really easy to check the employees' urine samples.

Answer 6: Gibberish Question

In stereo where available.

Yeah, you really don't get the true "Diff'rent Strokes™" experience unless you hear "What 'chu talkin' bout, Willis?" spoken in stereo.

And You Wonder Why They Call You a Loser

Which of the following is NOT a "Charlie Brown™" made-for-TV special?

a. "You're Not Elected, Charlie Brown™"

b. "It's the Easter Beagle, Charlie Brown™"

c. "It's Arbor Day, Charlie Brown™"

d. "It's a Grand Old Flag, Charlie Brown™"

Question 8

"Laverne & Shirley" Around the World

TV's Laverne and Shirley refer in Yiddish to "schlemiel" and "schlimazel." In plain English, what are they saying?

a a sausage and a ham

b a fool and a loser

c a drunk and a nymphomaniac

d a sister and a companion

Question 9

It's Not Polite To Talk with Your Mouth Full

They say if you're born into money, you're born with a silver spoon in your mouth. Suppose you were born with a "Silver Spoons™" character in your mouth. Whom of the following could you NOT have rubbing against your tonsils?

a Whitney Houston

b Jason Baseman

c Kirk Cameron

d John Houseman

It's a Grand Old Flag, Charlie Brown™ has never been made. There are already so many fine children's specials about Flag Day that they just didn't feel the need.

Answer 8

b A fool and a loser. They must be singing about Lenny and Squiggy.

Answer 9

C. KIRK CAMERON WAS NEVER ON "SILVER SPOONS™." YOU CAN TAKE A MOMENT TO GET THE IMAGE OF JOHN HOUSEMAN RUBBING YOUR TONSILS OUT OF YOUR HEAD.

Banged a Gong (Got It On)

Boinked or Didn't Boink?

1. Dave and Maddie

2. Lois and Clark

3. Mary and Lou

4. Sam and Diane

5. Jerry and Elaine

6. Joel and Maggie

7. Oscar and Felix

Didn't You Wear That Yesterday?

2. the Skipper

sweater

landlady

baseball cap

4. Boss Hogg

super

purple boa

5. Eddie Munster

thigh

paisley ascot

blue shirt

jester's hat

fatigues

7. Joanna Loudon

smokes cigars

teal poncho

vest

tip jar

1. Mork

white suit

black shorts

pink hot pants

3. Helen Roper

real hog's hide

leather jacket

turban

birthday suit

top hat

6. Dwayne Schneider

rainbow suspenders

muu-muu

see-thru halter top

DisOrDat Answer

1. **Dave and Maddie**/*boinked*
2. **Lois and Clark**/*boinked*
3. **Mary and Lou**/*didn't boink*
4. **Sam and Diane**/*boinked*
5. **Jerry and Elaine**/*boinked*
6. **Joel and Maggie**/*boinked*
7. **Oscar and Felix**/*didn't boink*

Jack Attack Answers

1. *Mork/ rainbow suspenders*
2. *the Skipper/ blue shirt*
3. *Helen Roper/ muu-muu*
4. *Boss Hogg/ white suit*
5. *Eddie Munster/ black shorts*
6. *Dwayne Schneider/ vest*
7. *Joanna Loudon/ sweater*

Rate Your Score

36 points or better: Succulent.
Much like Duck á l'Orange,
or Peking duck. Crispy duck is
pretty damn tasty too.

30–35 points: Mostly juicy.
Like a good quiche, we think.
But we're not sure what quiche is.

20–29 points: Undercooked in parts.
Imagine microwave fajitas.

10–19 points: Dry and raw.
Kind of like when they ate the
frozen people in that "Alive" movie.

0–9 points: Rump roast.
As in you just got your ass fried.

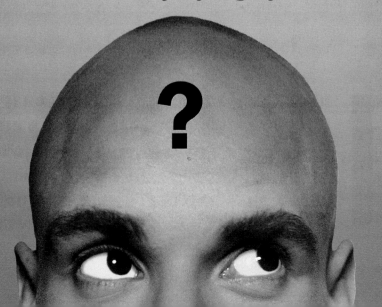

Game

6

Question 1
Will Date for Money

Which of these stars has never been a contestant on "The Dating Game™"?

a Arnold Schwarzenegger

b Farrah Fawcett

c Steve Martin

d Vanna White

Question 2

Free the Puppets!

Say you're a special agent hired to track down and exterminate puppets hiding out in the human world. On the set of which show would you NOT find any puppets?

a. "Unhappily Ever After"

b. "Soap™"

c. "ALF"

d. "3rd Rock from the Sun™"

Question 3

Saturday Morning TV that Makes You Go Blind

Which of these was an actual TV show?

a. "Pud's Prize Party"

b. "Playing with Peter"

c. "Dickie's Dial-In"

d. "Wee Willie's Winker"

d While she was a contestant on "The Price Is Right™," Vanna never made it on "The Dating Game™." They tried to put her on the show, but every time a stage light lit up, she'd start pushing on it.

D. THERE ARE NO PUPPETS ON "3RD ROCK FROM THE SUN™." OF COURSE, BEING THE SKILLED SPECIAL AGENT THAT YOU ARE, YOU KNOW YOU CAN'T BE SURE THEY'RE NOT PUPPETS UNTIL YOU STICK YOUR HAND UP THEIR BUTTS AND SEE IF YOU CAN MAKE THEM TALK.

"Pud's Prize Party" was a 1950s talent competition for kids. You don't even want to know the specific talent that was involved in the show.

Gibberish Question

With what phrase does this rhyme?

Flickernish Nosescum

Drill-kit buzz the knotty wood.

Hint **1**

It's an advertising slogan.

Hint **2**

The ad is for a type of drink.

Hint **3**

It comes from a cow.

Question 5

Making Vehicles for Vehicle Makers

If a U.S. car company decided to sponsor a non-fiction TV program, which of the following shows might you see?

a.
"Chevrolet™ Presents: 'Baretta'"

b.
"Dodge™ Presents: 'The Avengers'"

c.
"Chevrolet™ Presents: 'Nova'"

d.
"Ford™ Presents: 'The Thunderbirds'"

Question 6

NBC™ & THE VALLEY OF THE PHAT BEATS

Today's rappers should really give their props to former "Today" host Dave Garroway. Because he always closed the "Today" show this way, what phrase shows that Dave was "down for the real"?

(a) "Courage."

(b) "And we out."

(c) "Peace."

(d) "That's the way it is."

Milk. It does a body good.™

Yep, milk does a body good.
That's why you should bathe in it.

Answer 5

CHEVROLET™ HAD A CAR **CALLED A NOVA** WHICH IS ALSO THE NAME OF A PBS™ DOCUMENTARY PROGRAM. **BUT THE SHOW** EVERYONE'S WAITING FOR IS "YUGO™ PRESENTS: **PIECE OF CRAP."**

Answer 6

"Peace."

The simple phrase was the

signature closing line of Dave

Garroway, the original host of

"Today." But not before

sending a shout out to his

main man, DJ Fred Muggs.

MAKE-BELIEVE DOGS WISH TO THANK THE ACADEMY

Say the networks begin hiring cartoon dogs to do the news. Because the award named is an actual trophy for broadcasting excellence, which of these scenarios might occur?

- **a** Odie catches an ODIE.
- **b** Mr. Peabody fetches a PEABODY.
- **c** Rolf the Dog digs up a ROLF.
- **d** Droopy retrieves a DROOPY.

Across the Tracks from the Bradys

"Here's the story of a man named _____ who was friends with a junk dealer named Fred." What could you call this sitcom?

a.
"The Beatty Bunch"
b.
"The Grady Bunch"
c.
"The Hades Bunch"
d.
"The Shady Bunch"

You're Cooking with Crisco™ Now

If Swiss inventor Hans E. Laube's TV-related invention had been successful, what could viewers of "Yan Can Cook" have been able to do to enhance their viewing pleasure?

a. smell the simmering quail egg delicacy

b. ask Yan questions through the TV

c. tap Yan on the shoulder to get his attention

d. taste the Shanghai Duck Salad

Answer 7

b

The Peabody Award is considered to be the most prestigious in broadcasting, so Mr. Peabody from "The Bullwinkle Show," might win one. But scandal would hit when they found out about his "pet boy Sherman."

Answer 8

b

"The Grady Bunch." It's all about Grady Wilson from the show "Sanford and Son." Of course in this case, "Bunch" means "large stack o' hubcaps."

Answer 9

a

HANS E. LAUBE EXPERIMENTED WITH "SMELLO-VISION," AN ATTEMPT TO TRANSMIT SCENTS ALONG WITH SOUNDS AND IMAGES. AND IT WAS GREAT FOR COOKING SHOWS, UNTIL THE FIRST TIME WE SAW "YAN CAN CUT THE CHEESE."

Tonight, on a Very Special "Match Game™" . . .

Game Show or Sitcom?

1. "What's My Line?™"

2. "What's Happening!!™"

3. "What's Going On?"

4. "Anything for Money"

5. "Anything for Love"

6. "Babes"

7. "Studs™"

Jack Attack

What Makes You Different from Any Other Cop?

shoots self out of a cannon

2. "McCloud™"

paraplegic consultant

Buddy Ebsen

hippie cops

narcoleptic desk sergeant

4. "Longstreet"

black cop in rural South

robot partner

pregnant partners

6. "The Mod Squad"

bionic powers

blind investigator

transvestite police chief

Eskimo in Europe

comedy

1. "Ironside"

stripper by night

Dennis Weaver

cowboy in big city

3. "Cannon™"

teenage sheriff

lives on long street

never uses vowels

5. "Carter Country™"

vampire detective

perfume

overweight detective

7. "Forever Knight"

drives talking car

DisOrDat Answer

1. "What's My Line?™" / *game show*

2. "What's Happening!!™" / *sitcom*

3. "What's Going On?" / *game show*

4. "Anything for Money" / *game show*

5. "Anything for Love" / *sitcom*

6. "Babes" / *sitcom*

7. "Studs™" / *game show*

Jack Attack Answers

1. "Ironside" / paraplegic consultant

2. "McCloud™" / cowboy in big city

3. "Cannon™" / overweight detective

4. "Longstreet" / blind investigator

5. "Carter Country™" / black cop in rural South

6. "The Mod Squad" / hippie cops

7. "Forever Knight" / vampire detective

Rate Your Score

36 points or better: Very strong.
You could lift cinderblocks with that brain.

30–35 points: Sorta shapely.
Do you own an Easyglider™?
You could use a little more exercise.

20–29 points: Thin.
We suggest you keep your hat on at the beach.

10–19 points: Weak.
You've really let yourself go.

0–9 points: Flabby.
Call your local pharmacy.
They have drugs that can help you.

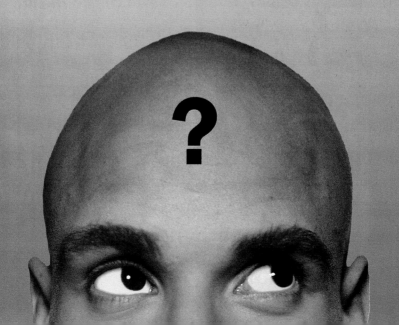

Game 7

Question 1

60 Minutes of Fame

If Andy Warhol had painted a silk-screen tribute to the TV show on which he appeared as a guest star in 1985, what image might art connoisseurs have seen?

a.
Gilligan at
"The Last Supper"

b.
Tootie's shoe

c.
repeated images
of Julie McCoy's face

d.
Tattoo on a
Campbell's Soup™ can

Question 2

BROUGHT TO YOU BY THE LETTERS CK™

Say Calvin Klein introduces a line of fashions designed to make you look like Bert from "Sesame Street™." Which of these accurately describes part of the ensemble?

a. a white T-shirt

b. a plain turtleneck

c. a red, blue, and yellow striped shirt

d. a navy blue cardigan

Question 3 — Ostentatious People & Their Large Jewels

Gibberish Question

With what slogan does this rhyme?

Why flaunt thy gem? Fee free!

Hint 1
Many musicians have said this.

Hint 2
It involves a cable network.

Hint 3
Wanna see a music video?

Answer 1

C Warhol was a guest on "The Love Boat," so we'd have a painting with numerous images of Julie McCoy.

Ahhhhhhhhhhhhh!

Answer 2

b

Bert always wears a plain turtleneck underneath his shirt.

And try new Calvin Klein™

Eau de Pigeon . . .

Answer 3: Gibberish Question

I want my MTV™!

Word is MTV™'s changing its name to "Real World Channel."

I'm a Little Bit Country

Congratulations! You've landed a chorus audition for the "Donny and Marie" show. Given the main attraction of the chorus, what should you bring to the audition?

a a ventriloquist's dummy

b ice skates and a pink tutu

c tap shoes, hat and cane

d flippers and goggles

Question 5

Not All Repairmen Show Crack

You've got a TV repairman out to look at your set because the picture keeps getting all snowy. If your repairman is from the "The Outer Limits™ Repair Shop," what will he MOST likely say?

a. "It's entered the fifth dimension."

b. "I can see 20 minutes into the future."

c. "It's smart. Very smart."

d. "There is nothing wrong with your TV set."

Question 6

You Take the Bad, You Take the Really Bad

Suppose the guy who wrote the theme song to "The Facts of Life™" serenaded the girls outside their window. What might we see next?

a Blair blowing a kiss to Alan Thicke

b Jo making eyes at Paul Williams

c Natalie dropping a love note to Weird Al

d Tootie skating away with John Denver

b

On the "Donny and Marie" show, the ice skating chorus was called the Ice Angels, formerly the Ice Vanities. Along with your ice skates and pink tutu, you might want to bring along a sign that says "Please Beat the Snot Out of Me."

Answer 5

d

When the screen goes snowy at the beginning of an "Outer Limits™" episode, a voice-over says: "There is nothing wrong with your television set. Do not attempt to adjust the picture." Of course, you'll still be billed for the service call.

Answer 6

BELIEVE IT OR NOT, THE THEME SONG TO "THE FACTS OF LIFE™" WAS WRITTEN BY "GROWING PAINS™" STAR ALAN THICKE.

YOU DIDN'T THINK IT WAS POSSIBLE TO DISLIKE ALAN THICKE MORE, DID YOU?

Question 7

They Only Make Little Green Cars

If you buy a Martian-made car with the same abilities as Uncle Martin from "My Favorite Martian™," what will happen when you raise the radio antenna?

a. Your car will disappear.

b. Your car will levitate.

c. All the other Martian cars will come to you.

d. You will be able to read other drivers' minds.

Question 8

TV DINNER GUESTS

If Chico from "Chico and the Man" invites you over for dinner, what might you say upon getting a friendly tour of his domicile?

a "Nice gearshift—manual or automatic?"

b "Cool junkyard. Nice and roomy."

c "I bet the fridge that came in this was nice."

d "So which part do the horses sleep in?"

Question 9

I've Seen the Future of Dating . . .

Say Maya from "Space: 1999™" goes on "The Dating Game™" to find a boyfriend. Considering their common unique ability, which bachelor should Maya pick?

a.
Bachelor Number One:
Captain Marvel™

b.
Bachelor Number Two:
Manimal™

c.
Bachelor Number Three:
Viper™

d.
Jim Lange, the host

a

YOUR CAR WILL DISAPPEAR. UNCLE MARTIN VANISHES WHEN HIS ANTENNA'S RAISED. JUST ONE MORE REASON TO BUY AMERICAN.

Chico lives in an old truck.

And oh, how nice . . .

he hung up a new pine air

freshener just for tonight!

Both Maya from "Space 1999™" and Jonathan Chase from "Manimal" can change into animals. So after their date when he tells you they were "rutting like crazed weasels," you know it's true.

Eight is Enough To Fill
Our Lives with Czars

Russian Czar,
Bradford Kid or Both?

1. Susan

2. Peter

3. Nicholas

4. Joannie

5. Tommy

6. Alexander

7. David

Mixing with the Help

Benson

Florence

2. Mike Brady

Marilyn

Sam

Mrs. Garrett

Tom Willis

Latka

4. Jessica Tate

Tony

Mary Richards

6. George Jefferson

Florida

Lurch

Mrs. Livingston

Consuela

Alfred *Thing*

1. Gomez Addams

Kimberly Drummond *Mr. Belvedere*

3. Willis Jackson

Alice

Uncle Bill

5. Cissy

Aunt Bee *Soap*

Maria

Mr. French

7. Batman™

DisOrDat Answer

1. Susan / *Bradford*

2. Peter / *czar*

3. Nicholas / *both*

4. Joannie / *Bradford*

5. Tommy / *Bradford*

6. Alexander / *czar*

7. David / *Bradford*

Jack Attack Answers

1. Gomez Addams / Lurch

2. Mike Brady / Alice

3. Willis Jackson / Mrs. Garrett

4. Jessica Tate / Benson

5. Cissy / Mr. French

6. George Jefferson / Florence

7. Batman™ / Alfred

Rate Your Score

36 points or better: Good job.
If you were a tree product,
you'd be rich maple syrup.

30–35 points: Decent.
More along the lines of an
attractive cedarwood door frame.

20–29 points: Nothing spectacular.
Like a pencil (not one
of those really good ones).

10–19 points: Not good.
Let's just call you "Woody."

0–9 points: Crappy.
Like toilet paper.

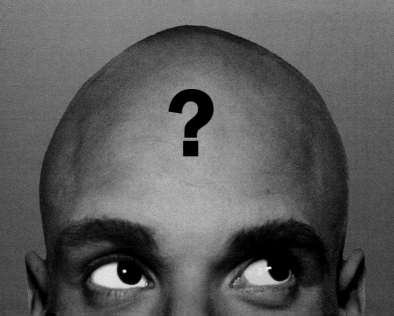

Game

8

Sharing the Laughter & Love with Damn Near Anyone

Suppose Maggie on "Growing Pains" divorced Jason, married "The Fall Guy™," then left him and married Ward on "Leave It to Beaver." If she kept the surnames in order, who would she be?

a. Maggie Seavers-Seaver-Cleaver
b. Maggie Seaver-Beaver-Cleaver
c. Maggie Seaver-Cleaver-Cleaver
d. Maggie Seaver-Seavers-Cleaver

Question 2

How Victor Kiam's Mind Works

Suppose you have Victor Kiam over for dinner. Based on his famous Remington™ electric shaver commercials, what might he do if he has a really good time?

a.
buy your house
b.
shave your head
c.
give you a football team
d.
burst into song

Question 3

JOHNNY & ED: THE EARLY YEARS

If Ed McMahon and Johnny Carson were reminiscing about the game show they first hosted together, what would Ed ask Johnny?

a "Who Do You Trust?"
b "Where Was I?"
c "What's My Line?™"
d "How's Your Mother-In-Law?"

Answer 1

d IN ORDER, THE "GROWING PAINS" FAMILY NAME IS SEAVER, "THE FALL GUY" IS COLT SEAVERS, AND "WARD" IS A CLEAVER. AND HER NEW SHOW WOULD BE CALLED "GROWING GUY PAINS BEAVER."

Answer 2

a According to the commercials, Victor Kiam liked the Remington™ electric razor so much, he bought the company! Just be sure he doesn't take a liking to your children.

Answer 3

a The game show was "Who Do You Trust?" And with all that "You may have just won a million dollars" crap, it's certainly not Ed.

Question 4

Playing the Organ

Suppose the Grinch™ renews his driver's license and becomes an organ donor. According to the song about him, what would the Grinch™ most likely hear if he's rejected as a donor?

a.
"Sorry, your heart is two sizes too small."

b.
"We'll need to remove the horn first."

c.
"We can't take your spleen—it's rotten."

d.
"Step to the back of the line, pinhead."

Question 5

AT LAST, DAVE THOMAS! I HAVE FOUND YOU!

Considering his name, Ben Vereen's character from "Roots" would make the MOST appropriate spokesperson for which fast-food chain?

a Jack in the Box™

b KFC™

c White Castle™

d Pizza Hut™

Question 6 — Quick Rastafarians

Gibberish Question

With what TV show intro does this rhyme?

Rasta man say, "Weeding pull it."

Hint 1
It's about a superhero.

Hint 2
He lives in Metropolis.

Hint 3
My, he's fast!

Answer 4

THE GRINCH'S HEART

WAS UNDERSIZED

UNTIL HE SPENT SOME TIME WITH THE WHOS.

AND BY THE HAGGARD LOOK

OF THE DUDE,

YOU PROBABLY DON'T WANT

ANYTHING TO DO

WITH HIS LIVER, EITHER.

Answer 5

Ben Vereen played the

irrepressible Chicken

George. He portrayed a full

range of emotions.

Or perhaps it was a

"free range."

Answer 6: Gibberish Question

Faster than
a speeding bullet.

Superman™.
He's the most powerful man on the planet
but he still struts around in blue tights.

All My Wives

Say the folks from "Melrose Place™" are on the game show "To Tell the Truth™."
When asked, "Will the real Mrs. Mancini please stand up?"
which of these Melrose women will stay seated?

a Sidney

b Amanda

c Kimberly

d Jane

Question 8

Mythical Bars

Trojans are to Greeks as Cheers™ is to:

a. Fenway Park™

b. Gary's Old Towne Tavern

c. Melville's Fine Seafood

d. Mom's Bordello

Question 9

. . . But Natural Blondes Have the Most Fun of All!

Say blondes really do have more fun. Which of the partners in "Cagney & Lacey™"
and "Starsky & Hutch™" are having the MOST fun?

a. Cagney and Hutch

b. Starsky and Lacey

c. Cagney and Starsky

d. Lacey and Hutch

b

Although they did sleep together for a brief period,
Michael Mancini never married Amanda. The problem, obviously,
was that Michael is just afraid of commitment.

Answer 8

B. JUST AS THE TROJANS AND THE GREEKS HAD A LONG RIVALRY THAT INCLUDED THE TROJAN WAR, CHEERS™ AND GARY'S OLD TOWNE TAVERN ARE ALL-AROUND NEMESES. WHO CAN FORGET THAT ONE EPISODE WHERE SAM FINDS A WOMAN IN HIS BED, ONLY TO HAVE THE GUYS FROM GARY'S LEAP OUT OF HER BELLY?

Answer 9

a In the two brunette and blonde crime fighting duos, Cagney and Hutch have the most fun. Yeah, they look like they're having fun but only their hairdresser knows for sure.

The Teacher Gave Me a C++

Computer Language or "Head of the Class" character?

1. Maria

2. Fortran

3. Cobol

4. Algol

5. Jawaharlal

6. Arvid

7. Simone

What Did You Call Me?

"Meathead"

2. Major Houlihan

"hot-to-trot"

"Piehole"

"Little Buddy"

"Dingbat"

4. Freddie Washington

"Gallon Jugs"

"Shortcake"

"Pinky"

6. Mike Stivic

"Boom Boom"

"Happy Days™"

"Barney"

"Hot Lips"

"Hawkeye"

"Half Pint"

1. Edith Bunker

"Sly"

"Little House"

"Mr. Kotter"

"Raj"

3. Joanie Cunningham

"Major Dad™"

"nurse"

5. Captain B. F. Pierce

"Hamhocks"

"Milquetoast"

7. Laura Ingalls

"Wingnut"

*"M*A*S*H™"*

1. Maria/*character*
2. Fortran/*language*
3. Cobol/*language*
4. Algol/*language*
5. Jawaharlal/*character*
6. Arvid/*character*
7. Simone/*character*

Jack Attack Answers

1. Edith Bunker/ "Dingbat"

2. Major Houlihan/ "Hot Lips"

3. Joanie Cunningham/ "Shortcake"

4. Freddie Washington/ "Boom Boom"

5. Captain B. F. Pierce/ "Hawkeye"

6. Mike Stivic/ "Meathead"

7. Laura Ingalls/ "Half Pint"

Rate Your Score

36 points or better: Fantabulous!

30–35 points: Extravagantual!

20–29 points: Amazingacious!

10–19 points: Spectaculaborous!

0–9 points: Triumphantastic!

*This rating scale brought to you
by boxing promoter Don King.*

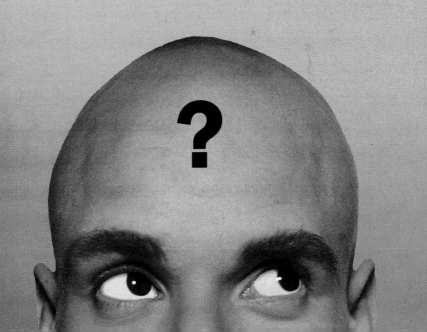

Game

9

Question 1

Not-So-Sweet 16

What did James of "James at 15" get on his 16th birthday?

- **a** a car
- **b** sex
- **c** marijuana
- **d** arrested

Question 2

At Least He's Not Named "Doogie"

Can you remember the name of this guy?

He's on "Growing Pains," he's Mike Seaver's friend, he's really stupid, and his nickname makes people giggle.

- **a.** Penis
- **b.** Dickie
- **c.** Boner
- **d.** Woody

Question 3 —Just for That, You Do the Laundry

Gibberish Question

With what phrase does this rhyme?

Snide Mike, you dry a towel.

Hint 1

It's something you'd say on "Wheel of Fortune™."

Hint 2

It's what you say when you don't want a consonant.

Hint 3

You can't have the vowel for free.

Answer 1

b On his 16th birthday, James lost his virginity to a Swedish exchange student. Lucky bastard. The closest most boys get to taking a Swede for a ride on their 16th birthday is borrowing their dad's Volvo™.

Answer 2

C. WITH A NAME LIKE BONER YOU KNOW HE'S THE WACKY NEIGHBOR. OF COURSE, THIS QUESTION IS REALLY JUST AN EXCUSE TO PRINT THE WORDS "PENIS," "DICKIE," "BONER," AND "WOODY" ON THE SAME PAGE.

Answer 3: Gibberish Question

I'd like to buy a vowel.

250 bucks for an 'e'?
Heck, you can pick up three 'o's and an 'a'
down at Kmart™ for $1.50.

CHEEK TO CHEEK

Think back to that touching made-for-TV movie "The Boy in the Plastic Bubble." Imagine that the "Plastic Bubble" is recycled into patio furniture, but they forget to take out the boy first. On whom would you end up planting your butt?

a) John Travolta
b) Shaun Cassidy
c) David Hasselhoff
d) Parker Stevenson

Question 5

What Would We Do, Baby, Without Guest Stars?

Uh-oh. The ne'er-do-well alcoholic Uncle Ned from "Family Ties" has gotten into the vanilla extract again. Considering the actor who portrayed Uncle Ned on "Family Ties," what might he say when Alex finds him in the pantry?

a.
"I like my vanilla shaken, not stirred."

b.
"Stupid is as stupid drinks."

c.
"Survey says . . . Vanilla!"

d.
"Definitely vanilla. Definitely vanilla."

Question 6

Hurry, Before the Commercial's Over!

Let's say you got a TV when it was first invented in 1926 and you refused to go to the bathroom until a commercial came on. How long would you have had to wait?

a. 1 year
b. 5 years
c. 10 years
d. 15 years

Answer 4

a

John Travolta played

"The Boy in the Plastic Bubble."

You know, it's a real drag when

your lawn chair is a better dancer

than you.

Answer 5

b Tom Hanks, a.k.a. Forrest Gump, riveted audiences as Uncle Ned on "Family Ties." An earlier version of the script has Alex finding out that his Uncle Ned is a cross-dresser who lives in a hotel for women.

Answer 6

d

THE TV WAS INVENTED IN 1926 AND THE FIRST AD WAS AIRED IN 1941. THAT'S 15 YEARS WITHOUT A BATHROOM BREAK. BUT ON THE BRIGHT SIDE—NO INFOMERCIALS!

Give Me Some Skin

Which of these characters would NOT set off the metal detector at the airport?

a **Michael Knight**

b **Twiki**

c **David Banner**

d **Steve Austin**

Question 8

HAIKU HI-Q

Name the TV character who might have written this autobiographical haiku poem:

Fonzie bangs jukebox
Potsie and Richie do sing
I sell place to Al.

a **Ralph**

b **Howard Cunningham**

c **Arnold**

d **Albert**

Question 9

Don't Kick Me There!

Which of the following pairs is NOT a match of a cartoon character and his sidekick?

a.
Boris and Natasha from "Bullwinkle™"

b.
Secret Squirrel™ and Morocco Mole

c.
Huckleberry Hound™ and Snagglepuss™

d.
Mr. Peabody and Sherman

David Banner, or the Incredible Hulk™, is not a machine or a rebuilt human being. He's just a regular guy who gets large and green when he's pissed.

Note to flight attendants: Give Dr. Banner an extra bag of peanuts to keep him happy.

Answer 8

ARNOLD, THE ORIGINAL OWNER OF ARNOLD'S. DON'T EAT THE BURGERS THERE, THOUGH. THEY'LL GIVE YOU THE CHACHIS.

Answer 9

C Huckleberry Hound™ and Snagglepuss™. They ain't partners, and they ain't friends. Word is, their relationship ended in an argument over which had the most annoying voice.

Three Men & the Red One

Wise Man or "Power Rangers™" Character?

1. Caspar

2. Goldar

3. Aisha

4. Zordon

5. Melchior

6. Balthazar

7. Trini

Old Actors Never Die; They Become Crime Fighter

1. Jed Clampett

"McCloud"

hairpiece

3. Sabrina Duncan

"Law & Order"

"Simon & Simon"

5. Andy Taylor

"TJ Hooker"

Klingons

"Magnum, P.I.

7. Mickey from "The Little Rascals™"

"Three's Company™"

"Mayberry RFD"

"Baretta™"

"Rockford Files™"

"Kojak™"

"Murder, She Wrote"

car commercials

2. Captain Kirk

"Our Gang™"

"McMillan & Wife"

"Barnaby Jones"

4. Archie Bunker

"Cannon"

"Scarecrow & Mrs. King"

"Mr. T & Tina"

"The Equalizer"

6. Bret Maverick

"In the Heat of the Night"

"Matlock"

"Murphy's Romance"

DisOrDat Answer

1. Caspar/ *Wise Man*
2. Goldar/ *"Power Rangers*TM *"*
3. Aisha/ *"Power Rangers*TM *"*
4. Zordon/ *"Power Rangers*TM *"*
5. Melchior/ *Wise Man*
6. Balthazar/ *Wise Man*
7. Trini/ *"Power Rangers*TM *"*

Jack Attack Answers

1. Jed Clampett/ "Barnaby Jones"

2. Captain Kirk/ "TJ Hooker"

3. Sabrina Duncan/ "Scarecrow & Mrs. King"

4. Archie Bunker/ "In the Heat of the Night"

5. Andy Taylor/ "Matlock"

6. Bret Maverick/ "Rockford Files™"

7. Mickey from "The Little Rascals™"/ "Baretta™"

Rate Your Score

36 points or better: Pretty good.
You need to work on your posture, though.

30–35 points: All right.
*It shows you don't have to be
attractive to know things.*

20–29 points: Average.
You don't always dress that way, do you?

10–19 points: Almost respectable.
*Perhaps the circus needs a new
sideshow performer.*

0–9 points: Sad.
You call that a hairdo?

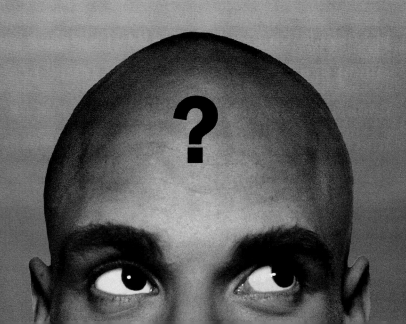

Game

10

Question 1

Hungry?

Complete this analogy:

Eve is to rib as Lamb Chop™ is to:

a. dam

b. mint jelly

c. sock

d. mutton

Question 2

BJ & Jane & Barney & Chico

Which of the following TV characters is accurately named?

a.
"Bear"
from "BJ and the Bear"

b.
"Cheetah"
from "Tarzan™"

c.
"Fish"
from "Barney Miller"

d.
"Man"
from "Chico and the Man"

Question 3

BECAUSE WE'RE SURE THE PUBLIC GIVES A CRAP

Say Phil Donahue hosts a show about his own marriage. Given his wife's most famous TV role, what would make the BEST title of the show?

a "'The Bionic Woman' Is My Woman!"

b "I Really Do Love Lucy!"

c "I Married 'That Girl'!"

d "'Alice' Lives with Me Now!"

117

Answer 1

C

JUST AS EVE WAS CREATED FROM A RIB, LAMB CHOP™ IS A HAND-PUPPET MADE FROM A SOCK. WHICH BEGS THE QUESTION—SHARI LEWIS: PUPPET GENIUS, OR JUST A REALLY BAD DRESSER?

Answer 2

YES,"THE MAN" WAS ACTUALLY A MAN. AND CHICO WAS QUITE CHEEKY AS WELL.

Answer 3

In 1980, talk show pioneer Phil Donahue married Marlo Thomas, the star of "That Girl." Of course, the show would probably achieve higher ratings if it were titled "I Married that Razor-Blade-Wielding, Leather-Wearing, Three-Armed Transsexual Girl."

I Feel Pretty & Fibber & Gay

If Ellen DeGeneres had come out of Fibber McGee's closet,
who or what would probably have come out after her?

- **a.** Genghis Khan and George Washington
- **b.** a whole lot of tumbling junk
- **c.** seawater and flopping fishes
- **d.** lies

And Now Here's Mary with the Weather

They say March is "in like a lion, out like a lamb." Judging by their personalities, which
of these pairs of "Mary Tyler Moore Show" characters best illustrates the same idea?

- **a** in like Mary, out like Murray
- **b** in like Ted, out like Sue Ann
- **c** in like Lou, out like Georgette
- **d** in like Phyllis, out like Rhoda

Question 6 — Did Russian Czars Get Much Tail?

Gibberish Question

What commercial phrase does this rhyme?

Sleaze won't tease a czar twin?

Hint 1
It's from a commercial
that began in the '60s.

Hint 2
The ad is for a brand of
toilet paper.

Hint 3
You're breaking Mr. Whipple's heart!

On "Fibber McGee and Molly," the TV version of the popular radio show,
Fibber McGee's closet is full of junk that tumbles out when he opens it.
Besides, in the '50s if Ellen said she was gay,
Fibber probably would say, "Gee, I'm glad you're feeling so happy."

Answer 5

**IN LIKE LOU GRANT, OUT LIKE
GEORGETTE FRANKLIN BAXTER . . .
OR "IN LIKE A GROUCH,
OUT LIKE A DINGBAT."**

Answer 6: Gibberish Question

Please don't squeeze the Charmin™.

Mr Whipple devoted his life to the protection
of toilet paper, which makes him a textbook
example of anal retention.

HE CAN STOP ANY TIME HE WANTS TO

Which of the following cereal spokesfigures exhibits "obsessive-compulsive" behavior?

a Mikey from Life™ cereal

b Cap'n Crunch™

c Sonny™, the Cocoa Puffs™ bird

d King Vitamin™

That Had To Be a Huge Placenta!

We all know where babies come from, but which of the following BEST explains where the ABC™ network came from?

a.
asexual reproduction by CBS™

b.
the love child of DuMont and DuPont™

c.
C-section performed on NBC™

d.
given up for adoption by the Air Force

They Came, They Laughed, They Died

Imagine there's a mass murderer prowling the TV production studios of old. Because it was the first show to use a live studio audience, which show could have been the first to end up with a dead studio audience?

a "The Honeymooners™"

b "I Love Lucy™"

c. "The Alfred Hitchcock Hour"

d. "Leave It to Beaver"

C

Sonny's constant thoughts about and hysterical consumption of Cocoa Puffs™ is a textbook example of obsessive-compulsive behavior. Some textbooks, however, simply list this as the "sugar-high" disorder.

C In 1941 the FCC ruled no one could own more than one network, so NBC™'s Blue Network was sold and became ABC™. Which explains how, to this day, Willard Scott just *knows* when Ted Koppel's in pain.

"I Love Lucy™" was the first show to be filmed before a live studio audience. But if the audience does turn up dead, Lucy's definitely got some splainin' to do.

Botany & Dodge City

Botanical Term or "Gunsmoke™" character?

1. Pistil

2. Festus

3. Stamen

4. Chester

5. Quint

6. Phloem

7. Kitty

But My TV Surname Is . . .

Payne

2. Roseanne Barr

Bundy

Taylor

Lincoln

Tripper

4. Mary Tyler Moore

Nanny

Fine

DeTusci

6. Fran Dresher

never has a last name

Morgan

Martin

Seaver

Johnson

Donner

1.Tim Allen

Cunningham

3. Martin Lawrence

Richards

Clooney

Huxtable

Micelli

5. Ellen DeGeneres

Quayle

Conner

Keaton

Torkelson

7. Tony Danza

Kedrick

DisOrDat Answer

1. Pistil / *botany*
2. Festus / "*Gunsmoke*™"
3. Stamen / *botany*
4. Chester / "*Gunsmoke*™"
5. Quint / "*Gunsmoke*™"
6. Phloem / *botany*
7. Kitty / "*Gunsmoke*™"

Jack Attack Answers

1. *Tim Allen/Taylor*

2. *Roseanne Barr/Conner*

3. *Martin Lawrence/Payne*

4. *Mary Tyler Moore/Richards*

5. *Ellen DeGeneres/Morgan*

6. *Fran Drescher/Fine*

7. *Tony Danza/Micelli*

Rate Your Score

36 points or better: Nice.
You look like a million bucks.

30–35 points: Not bad.
You look like twenty bucks.

20–29 points: Mediocre.
*If you save some money up,
you can have a shopping spree
down at the Everything's a Dollar store.*

10–19 points: Oops.
*You shouldn't have spent eight
bucks on a stupid trivia book
when you could have used it for
precious food.*

0–9 points: That's really bad.
You owe us money.

Other Uses for This Book

- **base for pick-up baseball games**
  (optional: crumble up page for ball, use brain as bat)

- **desk calendar** (dates not provided)

- drill a hole through it and use it as a record

- finally finish that **papier-mâché bust** of Wink Martindale

- get a bunch of them together,
  and use them as a path across shallow puddles

- heat it slightly, then sit on it

- hollow out for a wonderful **casserole dish**

- **kindling**

- place on head to **practice good posture**

- **wipe your boogers** on it

- short-term **life preserver**

- something to stick in a spare 5½" x 8½" frame
  you have lying around

- **throw at balls** stuck in trees

- buy two and use as platform shoes

- **chew toy**

- dietary supplement

- **noise device**—clip with clothes pin to your bicycle
  and it gives you that cool, motorized sound

- open it up, fan all the pages backwards,
  and you've got a **centerpiece** for a dining room table

- **something to cover carpet stains**

- **pillow** for unwanted house guests

- really **impractical hat**